Noah's Noisy Boat

Dave Hopwood & Nick Booth

This book is

Dedicated to

gorgeous Lucy!

All the illustrations

are by Nick Booth!

Also by Dave Hopwood:

The Big Bright Rhyming Bible – **Bible rhymes for little ones**

Telling Tales – **Interactive Bible stories**

See more at: **www.davehopwood.com**

© Dave Hopwood 2016

Here's a story with sounds really noisy,

Like **eek!** and **glug**

and

Scribberly

Okey-Dokey-Doo and Zippity-Zippity-Zipp!

and

Chippity-
Chippity-
Chip!

With **JIBBER JABBER JOO**

and Hissy

Wriggle too,

It's a noisy old book, and it's just for you.

God asked Noah to build a big boat,
To make it cosy and make it float.

If it sinks they'll be in big trouble!
They will all go

GLUG!

GLUG!

GLUGGLE!

So Noah gets a hammer and goes

BANG!

BANG!

BANG!

Then gets a spanner and goes

He gets a saw and goes

Zippity-Zippity-Zipp!

Zippity-Zippity-Zipp!

Zippity-Zippity-Zipp!

Zippity-Zippity-Zipp!

Zippity-Zippity-Zipp!

Gets a chisel and goes

Chippity-Chippity-Chip!

When he's finished he says

"Okey Dokey Doo!

My boat's Fine and Dandy!

Now what do I do?"

He gets some creatures with big swishy tails

That go

Swishity

Swish!

As the noisy boat sails!

He gets creatures that eat a lot

Chomple

Chomple

Chew!

And noisy ones that go

JIBBER
JABBER
JOO!

Crawling ones that go

Hissy

Hissy

Wriggleb

Funny ones that make Noah go

"Hee-Hee!

GIGGGGLE!"

Little tiny creatures going

Squeakity

Squeakity

Sque-e-e-ak!!

...and big wild ones that make Noah say

"EEEEEEK!!"

Lots of creatures on Noah's noisy boat.

He just hopes it will

Then it starts raining just like that!

PITTER-PAT!

PITTER-PAT!

PITTER-PITTER

PAT!

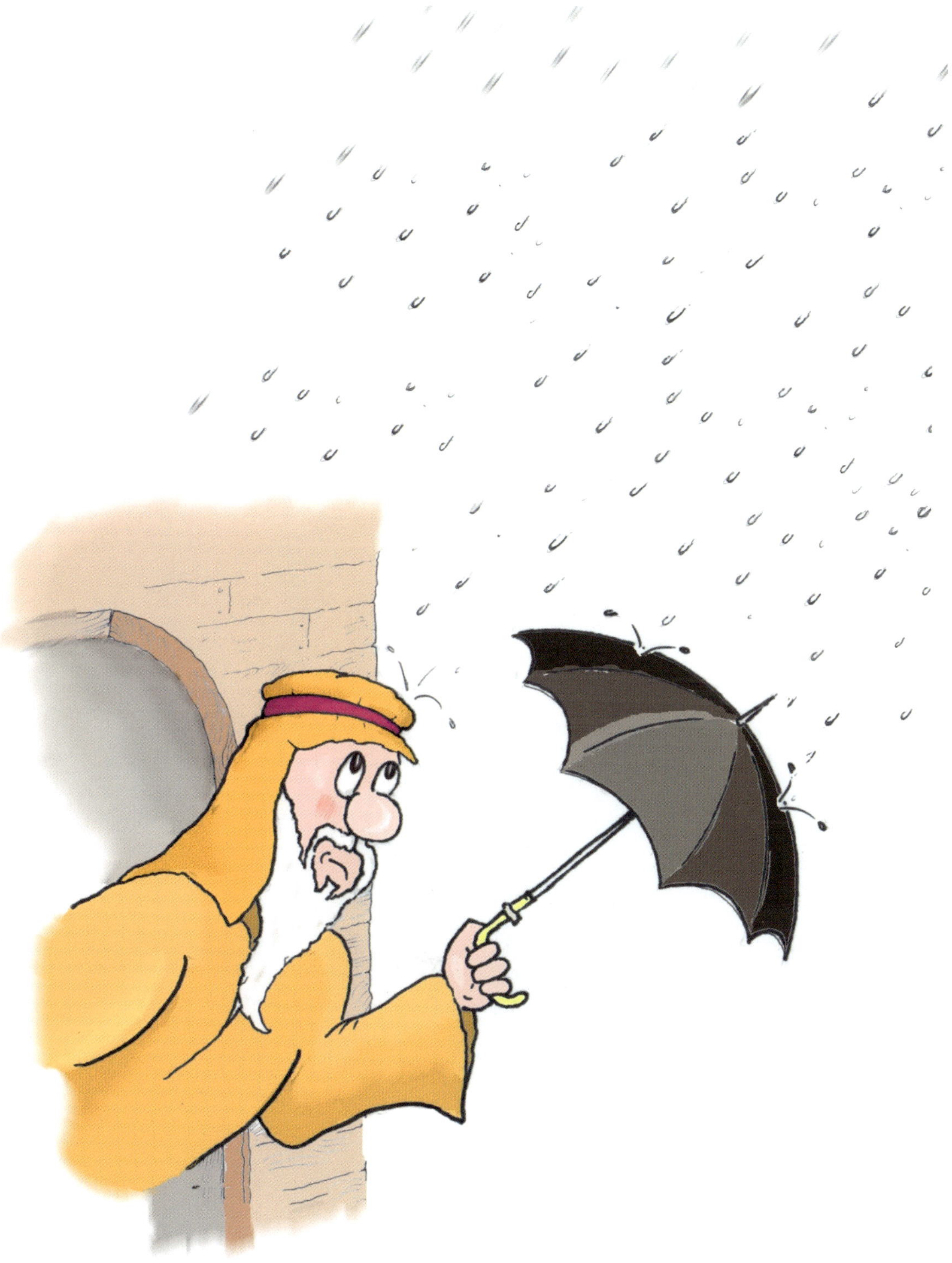

The waters rise up and make a

Splishy

Splashy

Sea!

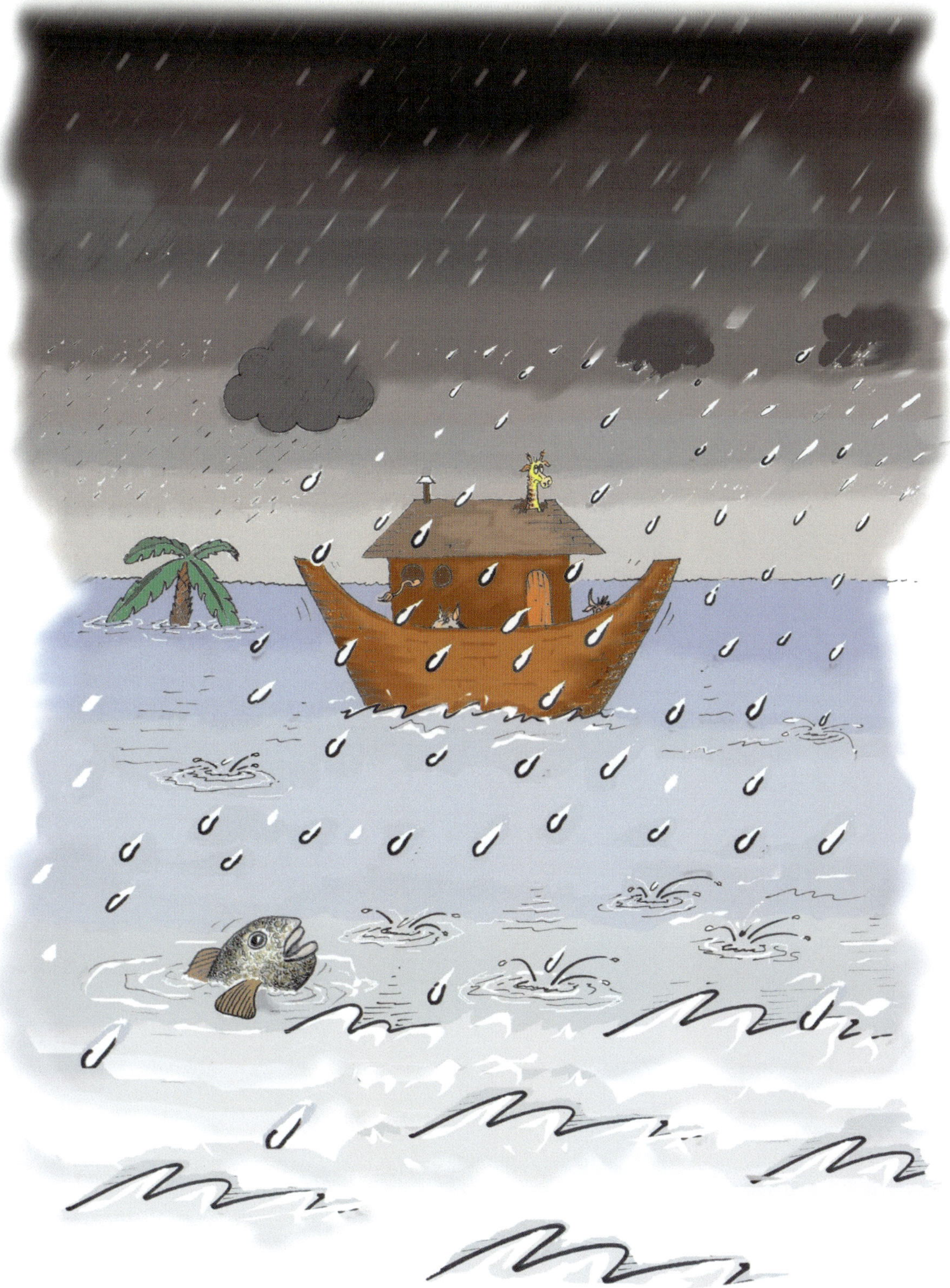

Looking like a line that is very

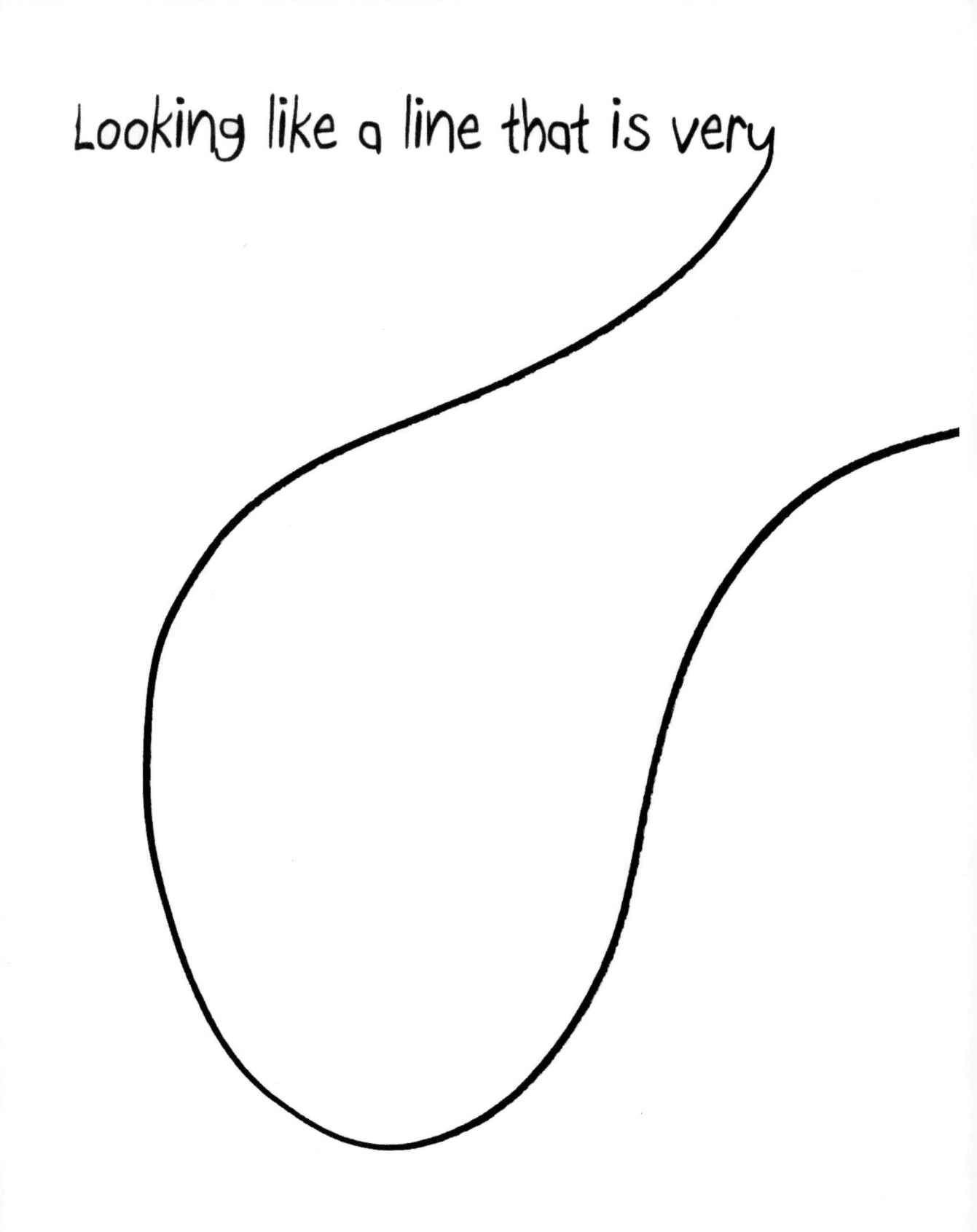

Scribberly

The boat goes up and down, and they feel a bit sick

Yuckity!

Yuck!

and

Ickity!

Ick!

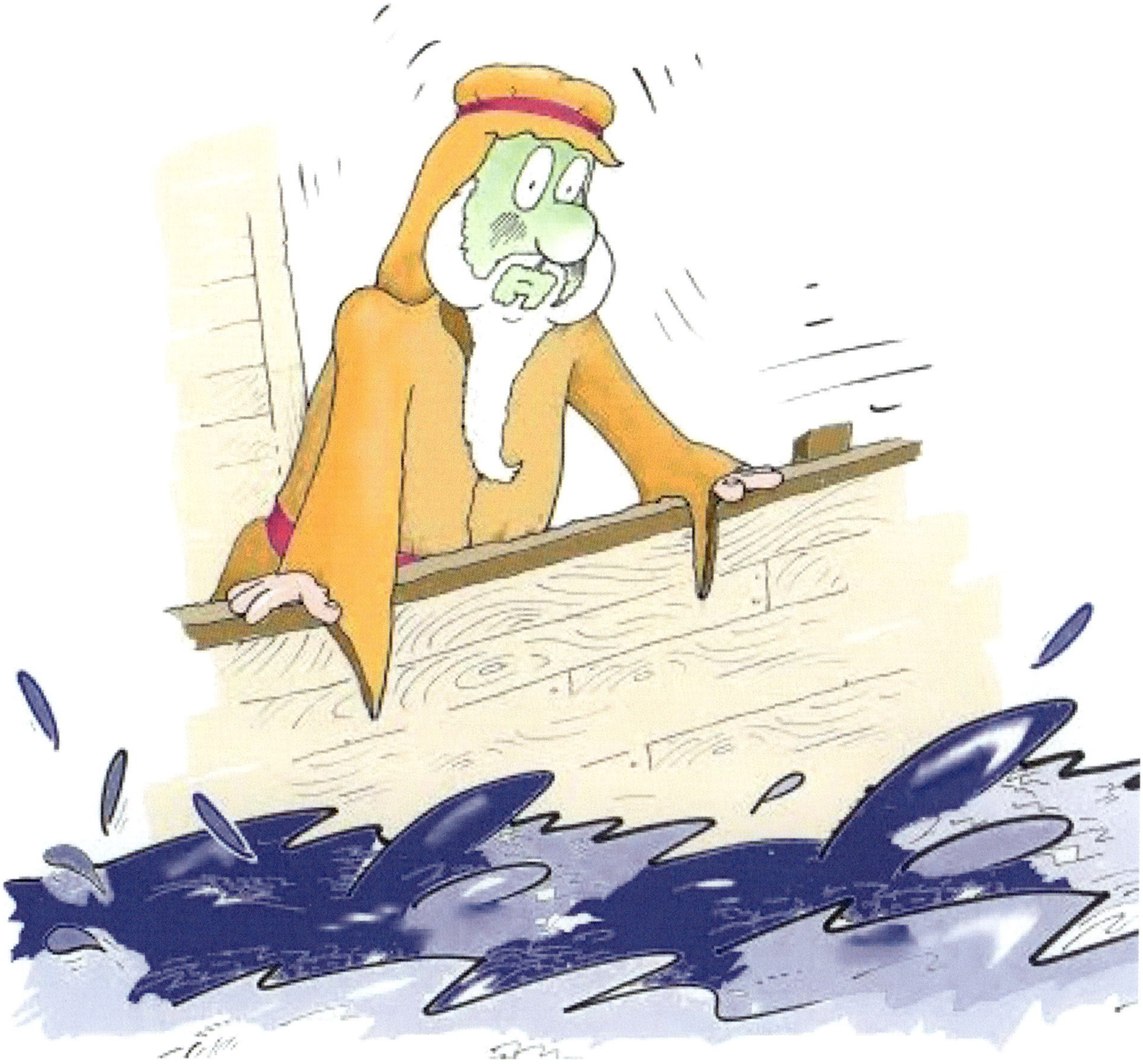

Then it goes quiet with a

Hushy Hush

Hussssssshhhhhhh!

The water runs away with a great big

Splussshhhh!

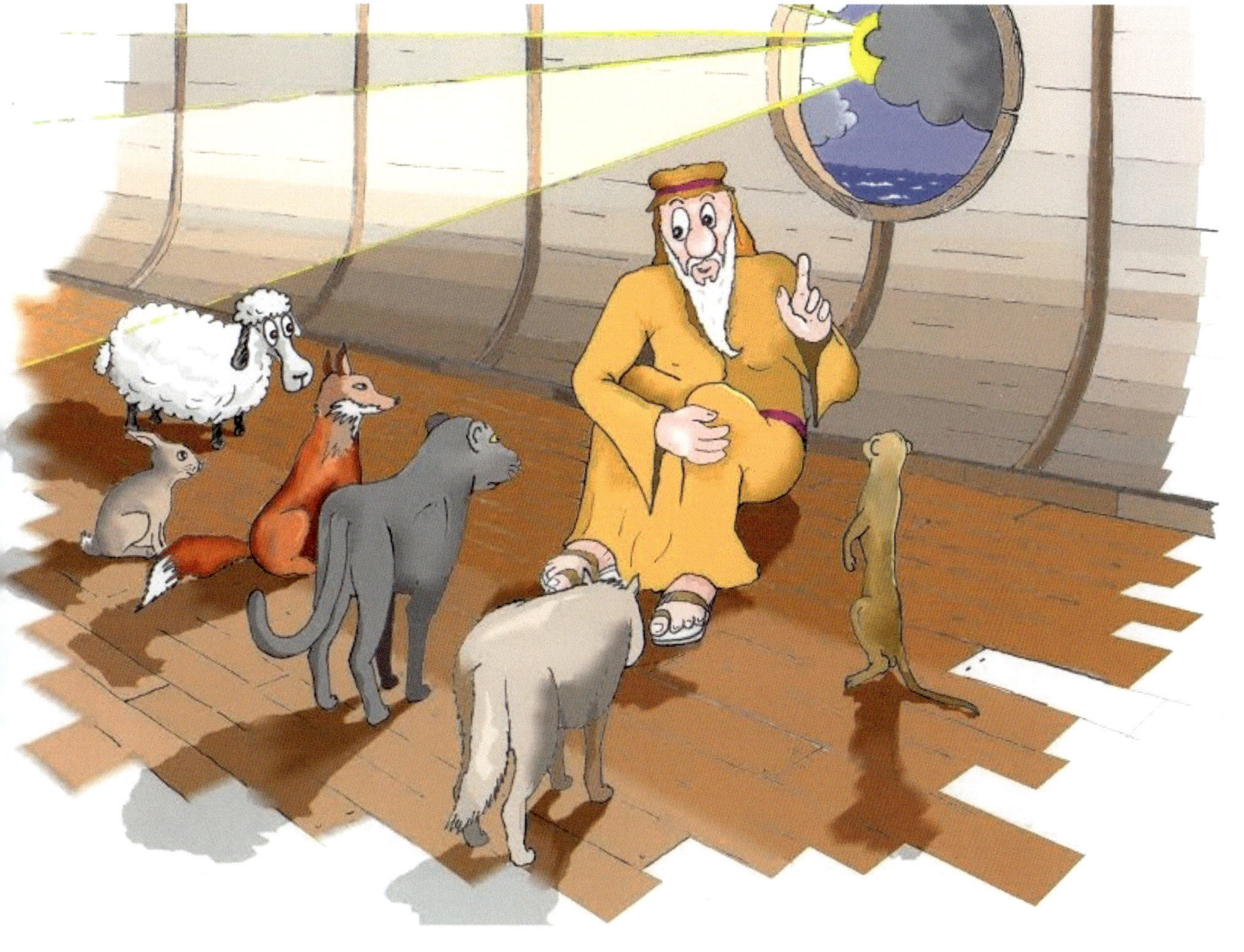

The world has had a wash –

SPLASH!

SPLASH!

SPLASH!

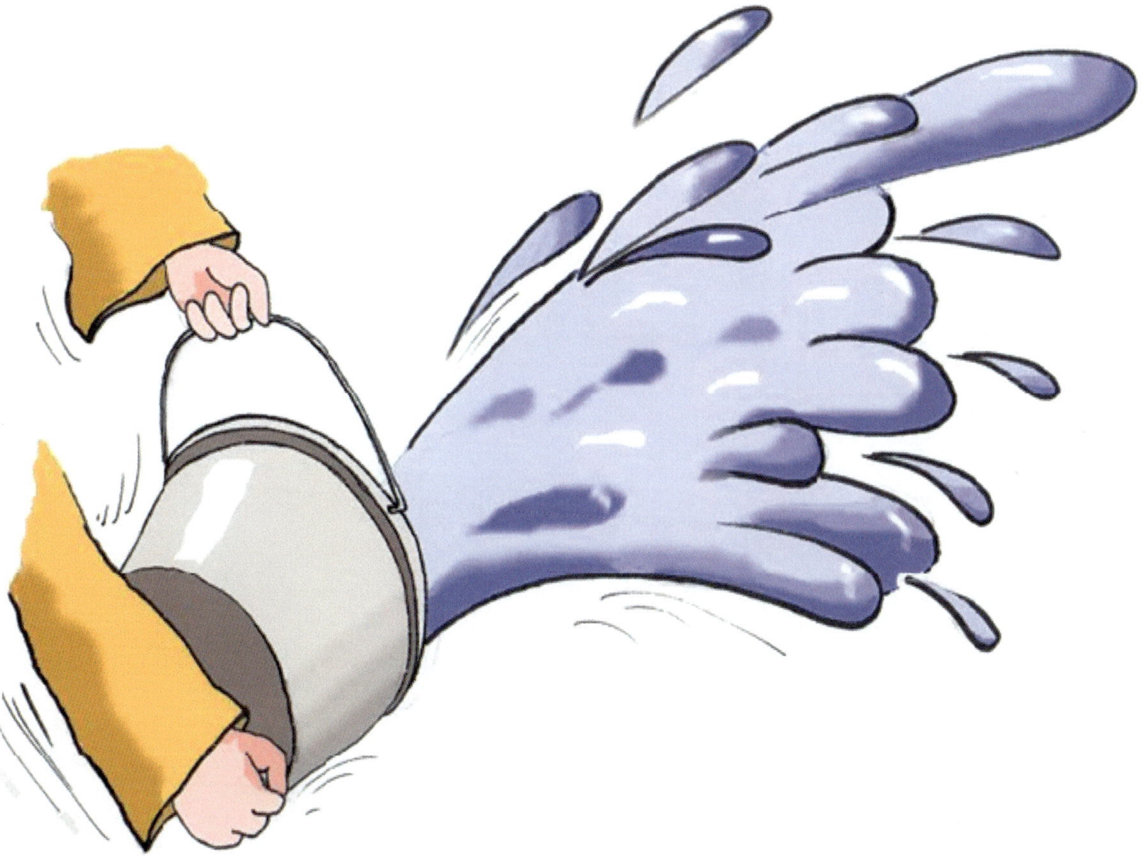

...and the animals come out going run! JUMP! DASH!

"Wait for me..."

The world has had a wash!

Hurray – it's looking better!

It needed a clean so it had to get...

...WETTER!

Everyone's safe in the

SHINY BRIGHT land,

So Noah builds a house with a

BANG!
BANG!
BANG!

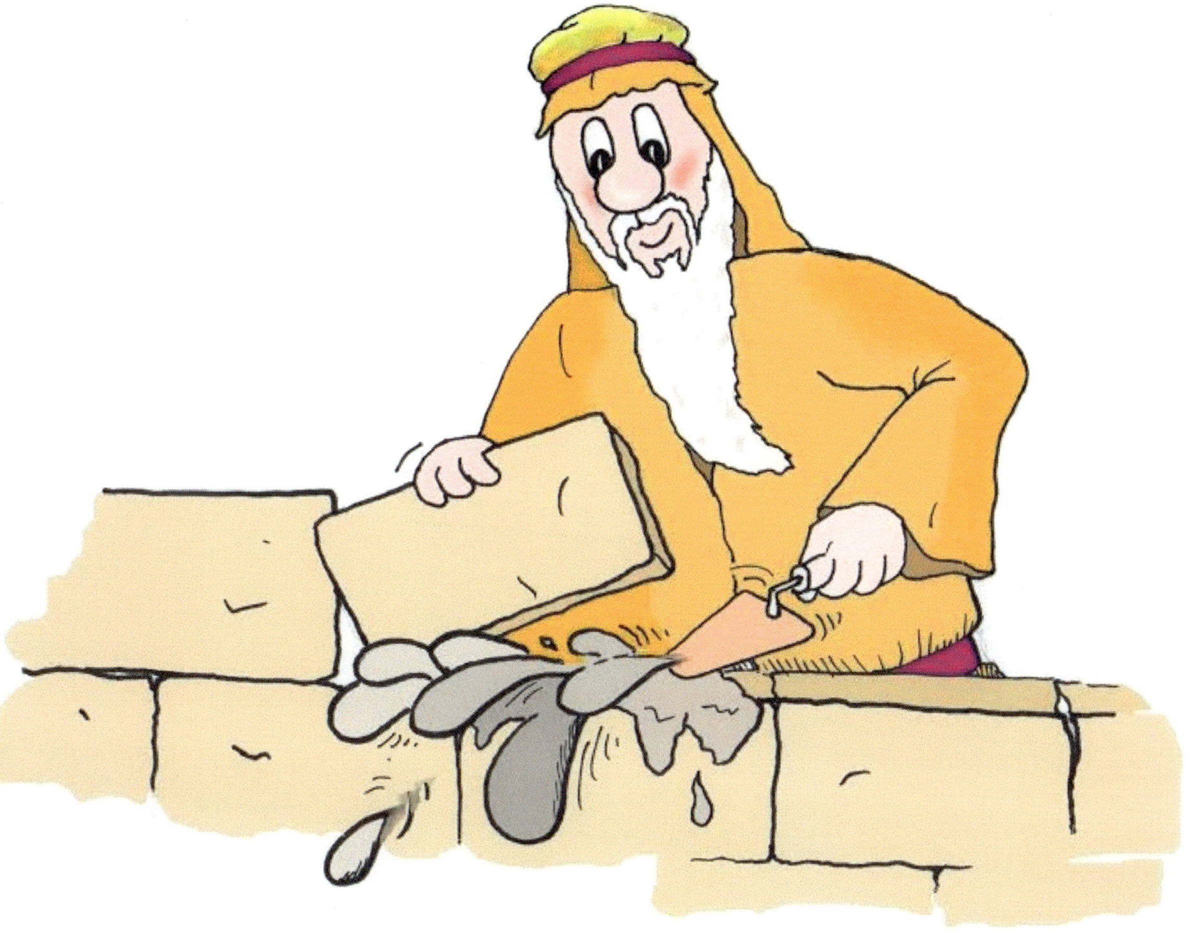

Then he gets a spanner and goes

CLANG! CLANG! CLANG!

And a big noisy digger going

Brum

Brum

Kerang!

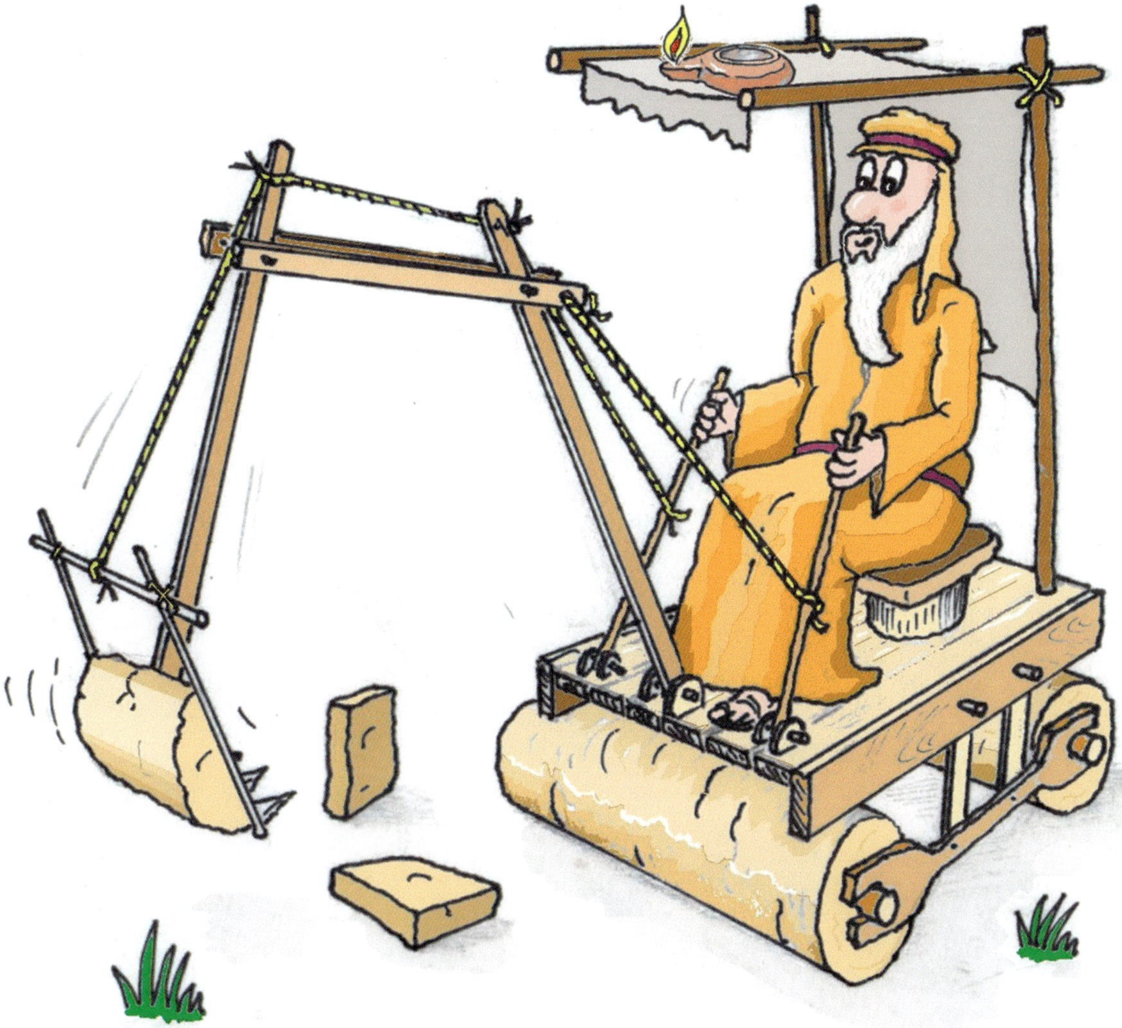

He makes everyone a home in the

SHINY BRIGHT
land.

Builds on **rock** not

Slippy sloppy sand.

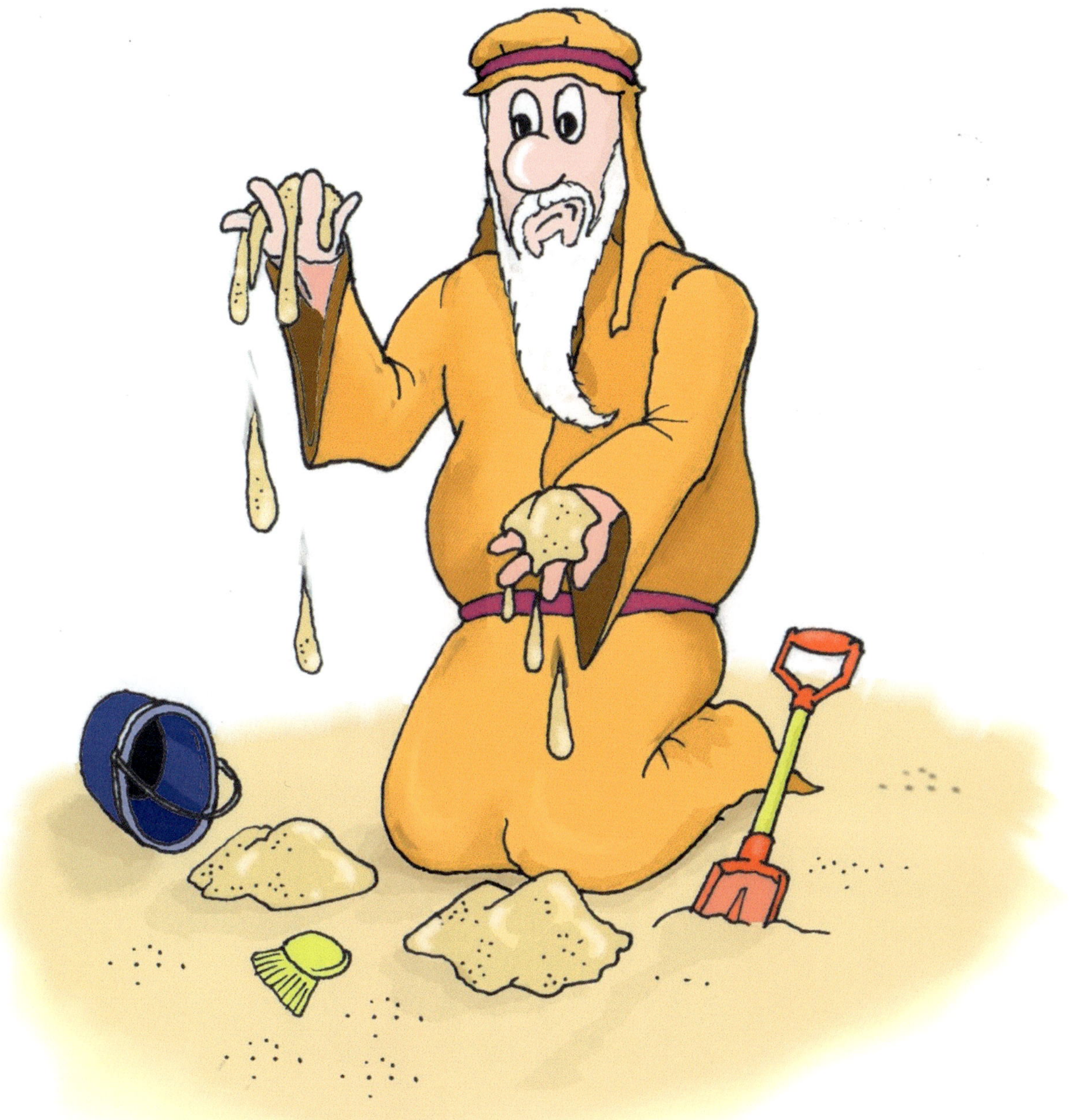

He gets a saw and goes

Zippity-Zippity-Zipp!

Gets a chisel and goes

Chippity-Chippity-Chip!

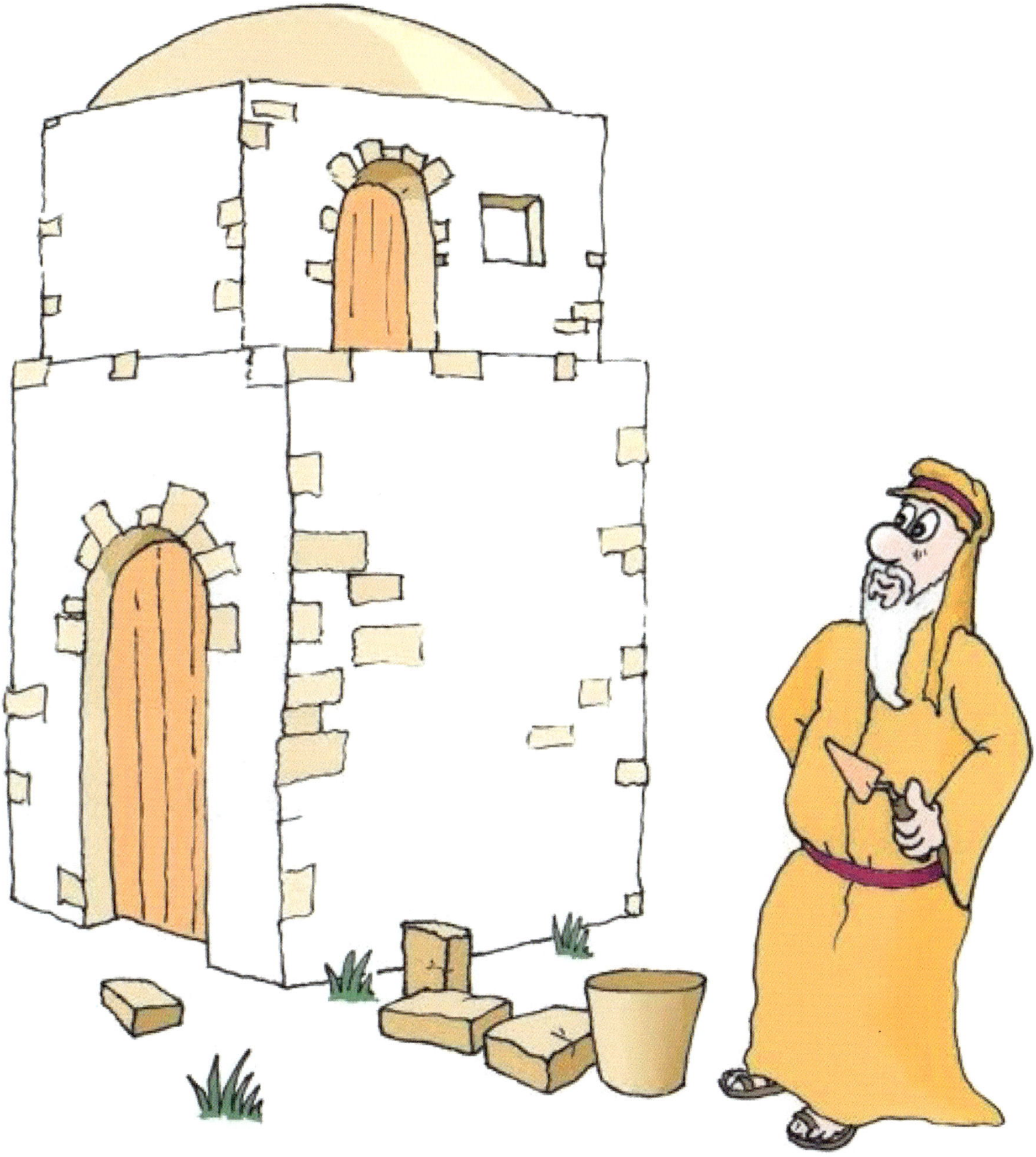

Then God sent a RAINBOW to light up the sky. It was multi-coloured and way up HIGH.

It was his way to tell everyone...

...he'd never FLOOd the earth like that again.

'You can read my story at the start of the Bible, in Genesis chapter 6 beginning at verse 9.'

Extra! Why not colour in Mr Beaver and paint your own rainbow?

Printed in Great Britain
by Amazon